T0107517

———— TELL ————

AMERICA

TELL
AMERICA

BY ANDY G. TRICULES

iUniverse, Inc.
Bloomington

TELL AMERICA

iUniverse books may be ordered through booksellers or by contacting:

iUniverse
1663 Liberty Drive
Bloomington, IN 47403
www.iuniverse.com
1-800-Authors (1-800-288-4677)

ISBN: 978-1-4759-5197-4 (sc)
ISBN: 978-1-4759-5198-1 (ebk)

Printed in the United States of America

iUniverse rev. date: 10/15/2012

DEDICATION

"TELL AMERICA" IS DEDICATED TO Judi, my wife of over 42 years, who has helped me assimilate much of the information contained in this book. Because of a medical handicap that she encountered eight years ago, many of her days are spent listening to and watching the news. The information that she has been able to glean daily has helped me immensely with assembling this book in its most simplistic fashion while keeping it user-friendly for my readers.

Educating America

I HAVE BEEN TRYING TO write this book for more than ten years and finally, due to what is currently taking place in our wonderful country, the time has come to tell America much of the truth and my perspective about our current affairs. My career started over four decades ago in the finance industry while I was attending college. I have witnessed several recessions and a number of turbulent events, but nothing compares to what has taken place over the past few years, especially with our economy. A day does not go by in which you don't read about or hear bad news via the media pertaining to foreclosures, increased unemployment, a rise in personal and business bankruptcies, and about millions of uninsured Americans struggling to survive.

Please keep in mind that this storm did not start last year; however, it has been brewing for more than a decade and is finally erupting. Our nation has been highly leveraged with debt that is currently into trillions of dollars and with several foreign nations who are now our creditors. Over the past forty years our beautiful land of milk and honey has gone from being the largest lender to becoming the biggest borrower as a nation. The truth is, as evidence will reflect, we have done it to ourselves and should manage up and take the blame and responsibility. The good news is that we are a very strong society and can bail ourselves out if and when we put our minds to it. Although it will not be a simple task, we will emerge if all Americans pull together in the right direction. By developing the right strategies and plans of actions that can be implemented and directed properly, there is no doubt in my mind that we will succeed.

Acknowledgements

1. Several of America's most prominent and wealthy business people who I had the great pleasure of working with many years ago taught me the following, "You can expect what you inspect. Since they gifted these powerful words to me, I've been inspecting many areas such as the U.S. economy, the environment, our government, and America's tax structure, in addition to health insurance. These are just a few areas that I have inspected and/or explored in our country, and was I rudely awakened as I started to research the overall impact they had on every one of our Americans. By the same token, I was able to share my findings with many of my friends and relatives, as well as my business associates. I have learned to share this inspection process with many people who I speak with daily, simply because they are clueless through no fault of their own.

2. Most people are busy going to work, paying their bills, and spending whatever spare and precious time they have with their family and loved ones. By the way, there is nothing wrong with this; however, I firmly believe that Americans should realize that they are working a good portion of their time in order to pay a variety of taxes and working the remainder of their time to pay themselves.

3. What about the fact that it will cost more than $250,000 to raise a baby today from birth through the age of 21, to adequately provide for them, which includes their college education. I'm sure you will agree that this is a sizable amount of money of which everyone should be aware and plan accordingly. Rest assured that both knowledge and valuable information such as this is priceless. As I have helped many people acquire this information over the past 25 years, my objective with this book is to educate the public and reader about much of what is going on today in our country and the major impact that these subjects and topics have on each and every one of us. I hope you enjoy the reading material as much as I have enjoyed writing about all of the areas you are about to explore.

Contents

TELL THE PUBLIC
THE TRUTH

M ORE THAN A CENTURY AGO our grandfathers and great-grandfathers were self-employed farmers, barterers, builders, and merchants. Our country later grew into manufacturing. Almost everything we wore, drove, and used within our households, from washers and dryers, irons, televisions, and photographic equipment to pharmaceuticals and drugs, were made in the U.S.A. In a nutshell, by the mid to late '60s we manufactured everything that every American could use daily. By the same token and during that same time, unemployment was very low, and our country was not leveraged and our level of stress was far lower than what it is today. Manufacturing and farming were the grassroots and backbone of our nation for many decades. Where has all of this gone and why did it happen so quickly and before our own eyes? It seems that today farming and growing our own crops is a thing of the past with literally thousands of farmers no longer in the farming industry. Also, millions of the same American jobs have disappeared as a result of many products and goods being produced in China, Taiwan, the Philippines, and other foreign countries. Where have we gone wrong, I keep asking myself.

I remember riding in my dad's American-made cars, watching a TV made by Zenith or Emerson, two very good U.S. companies, and wearing my good old clothing made in the U.S.A. Looking back in time, I recall all of these products being well made and lasting. So what changed all of this? Obviously, we out-priced ourselves by paying high wages to workers in the manufacturing environment and were undercut by workers from a number of foreign countries that could produce a similar product and could deliver the goods at a lesser cost to the American consumer. Much of our demise has been caused by unionization that demanded higher wages for our people, resulting in higher product prices, in addition to what we pay for the cost of advertising and distribution. Our competitors overseas immediately saw this and took advantage of the situation, delivering, in many cases, a superior product to the consumer for far less money. However, there is no reason to panic since we can regain our dominate position by implementing the right practices in order to reclaim our stake. As a good example: About eight years ago a foreign auto plant was opening in the southwest region of the U.S. and was in search of a few thousand production workers. The word on the street was that this foreign automobile manufacturer would hire non-American workers because our citizens would not work for $10 per hour. Much to the surprise of many, this company hired many American workers who did in fact come to work for $10 per hour, while the remaining employees from outside the U.S. followed suit. This proved the point that Americans will come to work for $10 per hour and perform their best with hopes that they will advance in the company. In short, Americans will work for less money if the opportunity is right for them and provides long-term potential for advancement. Corporate America offered such opportunities for many years and retained good talent, and in many cases the employees stayed with the company until retirement. Looking back in time and not that long ago, high school seniors were slated to go into some type of trade such as becoming a mechanic, plumber, electrician, or air-conditioning specialist while another group of seniors were targeting business opportunities and the remaining sector of seniors was bound for college to become doctors, lawyers, engineers, accountants, etc. This seemed to be the model until the late '70s. Shortly thereafter it appeared that everyone was encouraged to go to college and get a formal education. This made some sense at the time since our nation was shifting from a manufacturing environment to an emerging service industry and we were requiring more highly educated people versus trade workers. The dilemma that we're faced with today resulting from that paradigm shift is that we have an abundance of over-qualified highly educated people and a shortage of trade specialists. I personally don't know of many electricians, plumbers, air-conditioning specialists, and mechanics looking for work today. In fact, we have a shortage of people employed in trade industries such as truckers, heavy-duty equipment operators, and other types of tradespersons. I firmly believe that our future is based on rebuilding manufacturing facilities and developing more skilled people entering the trades. It is probably best to encourage every high school graduate to pursue both a formal education as well as some sort of trade profession. The point is that if and when you graduate from college and cannot find work in your given area of expertise at least you could work as a tradesperson and earn a decent living until the day your ship comes in with respect to finding employment commensurate with your college degree. All in all, this makes good sense and gives you a great backup position while covering all of your bases. I'm sure that you will agree that the moment is right to implement this type of strategy so that we can once again put most of America back to work and salvage our country. The time has finally come to open more vocational schools just as we had some 40 years ago and help train more of our American youth prior to entering a much-diversified work force. In summary, we need to communicate frequently and consistently with our congressional representatives and senators to further promote this educational process, as well as rejuvenate farming and manufacturing once again. Our timing is critical and we should act now.

II

An Oblivious Society

T HROUGHOUT THE PAST FEW YEARS and on a daily basis I have spoken to hundreds of people during my travels and activities and have come to the following conclusion—the vast majority of our population is somewhat oblivious to many of the economic events taking place in our nation. Although we are a highly educated and an academic society, we lack a great deal of common sense. Here's an example: Recently while pumping gas into my automobile a woman on the opposite lane pumping fuel said to me, "Isn't this great that gas is now $3.50 per gallon as compared to $4.00 per gallon recently and in 2008?" My response to her was to point out that Exxon/Mobil announced that they had a $41 billion profit in 2008 in spite of the high prices. I also pointed out to her that the price of gas was $.28 per gallon in 1962, and that it was more than $4.00 per gallon a while back. Both Exxon/Mobil could probably not show us a quarterly result over the past 50 years in which they lost money or just broke even. In essence, I'm certain they have enjoyed positive earnings every quarter for the past 50 years. I was also merely trying to explain that even if we were paying $2.50 at the pump that the oil companies would still be profitable. She thanked me for the brief dissertation on oil companies and how they are profiting off the American consumer and for bringing her up to speed on this reality. Unfortunately, many American consumers are not aware of these practices until someone brings this situation to their attention.

In yet another example, most Americans are not familiar with our health insurance and pharmaceutical programs. In 1998 my son came down with a very unique hip infection and was hospitalized at Wolfson's Children's Hospital in Jacksonville, Florida, for seven days in order to identify and cure the infection. Upon his release, the doctor wrote a prescription for a certain medication. On the way home we stopped at our local pharmacy to pick up the prescription. As I waited in the car my wife went into the store. She came out after a few minutes and suggested that I come inside to talk with the pharmacist who told me that this prescription would cost me $115 for a 14-day supply. He also suggested that we call the doctor that prescribed this drug and request a generic equivalent. My wife did so when we got home. Several hours later on my way home from work I stopped back in to pick up the drug. When I got to the drug store the prescription was ready for me at a cost of $10 compared to $115 earlier in the day. I asked to speak with the pharmacist and he explained that both drugs had the identical ingredients and with no variation. The key difference was that the drug for $115 had the letter B written on each tablet representing a certain pharmaceutical company that will remain nameless, while the other tablet had nothing written on it and was a generic drug. He assured me once again that both drugs had 100 percent identical ingredients and that it would not harm my son to take the generic version. I was truly shocked at the price difference of $105; however, this goes on every day and most Americans are not aware of this type of situation. To further prove my point, I challenge anyone to review financial statements of any pharmaceutical company, the vast majority of them being in the state of New Jersey, and show me any one of these companies that have not shown a profit for the past 40 years. Chances are that you will not find one.

The most critical area in which Americans lack knowledge is with respect to a significant paradigm shift that has taken place during the past few years causing many people to work from their homes as compared to the traditional workplace. In the years 2008-2010 more than 25 million Americans filed 1099 tax returns relative to working a home-based business. Allow me to put these figures into proper perspective. Out of a total U.S. population of over 300 million people, the figures show that roughly 180 million Americans are working in some way, shape, or form. We have 25 million out of 180 million American workers, representing almost 15 percent of our working population, working from their homes and the number is growing. I am sure you will agree that this is a pretty significant percentage of close to one out of every seven Americans. These people work in several of the following areas—direct sales, telemarketing, customer service, medical billing, child day care, insurance, recruitment, surveying, appointment setters, and so on. These are just a few areas in which people can earn a very good living without traveling daily to and from work and spending money on gas, lunch, wardrobes, and other miscellaneous expenses. This type of work practice will only increase since traditional jobs are falling by the wayside and decreasing by millions. More than 300,000 mortgage brokers that were doing well five and six years ago are struggling today to make ends meet. The same holds true for thousands of stockbrokers, Realtors, auto salespeople, insurance employees, and the like. According to a number of well-known economists it will be several years before all of these industries bounce back. Additionally, autoworkers, bankers, engineers, accountants, and other similar employees will fall into the same category. Unfortunately, the vast majority of these jobs will not be replicated; therefore, people will be forced into becoming entrepreneurs or exploring other industries and opportunities. All in all, home-based businesses will continue to grow and expand. Our fellow American typically becomes a believer in this paradigm shift once they become unemployed, typically having only two weeks of cash reserves on hand. However, while they're gainfully employed they don't really think much of this. In the back of their minds there is somewhat of a fear factor, yet it doesn't really hit home with them until they are confronted with a real pink slip. Once that occurs they truly understand. Just to summarize, I find that in talking with many people from all walks of life on a daily basis that probably 5 out of 10 do not have a handle on what is taking place in our country, despite the newspaper, TV, and radio media that deliver this information 24/7 to the public. It appears that people have a much better understanding once they are unemployed and have a major loss of income. It is unfortunate to say, but people truly react only when their personal pocketbooks are affected. Generally speaking, until this occurs they are just going with the daily flow. Let's not place blame solely on them since the media via TV, radio, and hard print is delivering a certain message to them and they feel compelled to act as believers, assuming that the information being conveyed to them is accurate. In many instances and much to their surprise, it isn't. Not to insult any of my fellow Americans, but it appears, after speaking to a number of people on a daily basis, that they don't have a real handle on what is taking place in our country. It would behoove them to acquire more of this knowledge so that they can better prepare themselves for the future.

III

LOBBYING AT ITS BEST

TODAY WE HAVE WELL OVER 15,000 lobbyists in Washington representing special interest groups. The number of lobbyists since President Bush's election and his inauguration in 2001 has increased dramatically. The $64,000 question is why has the number of lobbyists grown so drastically in the past decade? Just to put things in their proper perspective, we have 435 elected representatives in our House of Representatives. If you analyze this and do the math it appears that we have about 35 lobbyists for each representative. Why, and what does this mean? It clearly explains why certain bills are passed or not passed, and why our nation is in such despair.

First of all, all lobbyists have their own personal agendas and are out to exclusively represent a specialized industry such as the oil, pharmaceutical, and insurance industries, just to name a few.

All in all, each lobbyist's objective is to persuade every congressional representative and U.S. senator to see things in the same fashion that their represented industries see and feel about the beliefs of the business line represented. In the vast majority of cases, the consumer, such as you and I, are not in a winning situation. The only people that truly benefit are the lobbyists and the industries and companies they represent. Very rarely will you see a win/win situation in which all parties benefit.

At the end of the day our objective should be to eliminate special interest groups so that we as consumers have a level playing field and there is no bias from lobbyists and the industries they represent, as well as from our representatives that we have elected to serve us. Please don't misunderstand me. I believe that certain industries need representation for good causes that can ultimately help us; however, in the vast majority of cases, lobbyists are not needed to do so.

Lobbying, as well as unionization, served a very good purpose when they were originally formed; however, as time went by both lobbyists and unions did very little to truly serve their membership or the general public. The playing field should be equal between all Americans and our congressmen and senators that are supposed to represent the American public, and particularly those that elected them versus special interest groups who have their respective industry or client's best interests at heart.

The time has come, especially in these difficult economic times in which we as the American public who truly suffer from high unemployment, foreclosures, the lack of medical coverage, high educational costs, and so on should require and position our lobbyists to represent us in Washington with a greater degree of intensity.

This process can help us to start correcting the many problems and issues that we face daily. It appears that America does not have a strong enough voice in Washington among our congressmen and senators; therefore the level of urgency just isn't there. Once again, it is very difficult for us to compete daily with 15,000 plus lobbying voices and the high degree of favoritism toward those special interest groups. Rest assured that if we were in the faces of our representatives in Washington more frequently, and with good strategic plans of action, many of the problems facing America today would be minimized, streamlined, and corrected in the vast majority of cases versus continuing to linger without a solution or resolution.

Finally, it is of the utmost importance that we as hard-working and caring Americans, regardless of race, creed, or color, band together so that we can put this process in motion as soon as possible and forge ahead.

IV

OUR CURRENT TAX STRUCTURE

WHEN YOU LOOK AT OUR Federal income tax structure I'm certain that most of you will agree that it is very complicated and could be simplified so that every American citizen can understand it.

First and foremost, and for those of you that don't know, the Internal Revenue Service, better known as the IRS, employs more than 100,000 people in multiple locations throughout the U.S. When you think about this, just to make a comparison, several cities in our country have a population similar in size to the IRS. Now, let's factor in the number of buildings that they occupy and the infrastructure they require to operate day-to-day business, not to mention all of the other expenses such as the huge payroll expense included in the entire IRS budget. Please rest assured that this financial figure is huge and is laid on the backs of every American worker and taxpayer.

You must think and say that there has to be a better way to operate this process, and there is. If you look at several foreign countries and how their tax programs are designed you will find that they are much simpler in nature and easier to understand. They generally have a few tax forms to prepare and file and in the most elementary fashion. Here is an example: Let's say that you earn $50,000 per year. With a 10 percent fixed percentage tax plan you only pay $5,000. The same holds true if you earn $100,000 or $200,000. Your tax burden, once again, is $10,000 or $20,000, respectively, equating to 10 percent of your gross income. Pretty simple, isn't it? So why have we overcomplicated our system to the point of designing and having dozens of different tax forms to complete, not to mention what it costs the average American to have their income taxes prepared every year. The topic of different tax brackets, itemized deductions, exemptions, tax credits, contributions, and so on creates a nightmare when preparing a return, not to mention the room for error.

Modifying and streamlining this process would create a more effective tax structure for every American to understand and follow, as well as minimize effort in the preparation, and at the same time reduce stress. Here are some pros and cons. A major pro is that you can probably administer this entire process with just a few thousand IRS agents and other staff members versus the current IRS staff of more than 100,000 employees or so. Just think of the cost savings of reducing this staff to far fewer employees. Another pro is the elimination of much of the real estate that they occupy, the reduction of infrastructure, and the reduction of expenses affiliated with our current and existing Federal income tax program, thereby creating a simple process that involves preparing and submitting one document to the IRS. The last pro relates to simplicity, accuracy, and timeliness for filing purposes. Now let's examine the cons. More than 95,000 IRS employees would have to seek other employment. Tax preparation companies, such as H & R Block, would be adversely affected. Other accountants and tax preparers would not be necessary to assist with current and traditional income tax preparation, meaning their positions would be in jeopardy and/or eliminated.

I realize that all of this sounds terrible; however, should we continue to endorse a system that is faulty and very costly to every American taxpayer to support on a daily basis? Speaking on behalf of most fellow Americans, I am certain that almost everyone would support this change for the betterment of our system, as well as our great nation.

This subject has come up relative to a simple straight percentage tax structure by several of our past and current legislators. Unfortunately, with very little traction, this suggestion didn't get very far. It is time for America to do a hard press on this proposed modification in order to simplify the entire tax filing process for every American taxpayer.

V

DEALING WITH OUR ENERGY CRISIS

ABOUT 30 YEARS AGO I was traveling back to my home in New Jersey from a business trip in Detroit and had the great pleasure of flying alongside a Vice President of one of the top three auto manufacturers. Since our flight was a few hours long we had the opportunity to discuss several topics relating to automobiles. I asked him whatever happened to the auto being tested that could run on acid products such as orange juice, pickle juice, or another acidic type product or chemical. He smiled and responded that this concept-type vehicle had been aborted since it would have a major impact on the oil and auto industries. He also mentioned how strong the oil lobbyists were in Washington and what influence they had on congress and the senate. I responded to him by saying what a pity this is, especially since this would have been a great alternative to traditional fuel for autos, as well as for every American driver.

The point here is that for the past three or four decades we could have developed several alternatives to our existing fuel model if we put our minds and hearts into it. After all, we put man on the moon in the late '60s, enhanced computer technologies, and performed a number of other challenges far beyond our own beliefs. Today we're finally addressing other alternative methods of energy, yet we should have been pursuing these options more aggressively since the first gasoline crisis back in 1973-74. Obviously we didn't and were confronted once again back in the late '70s and early '80s. Here we are more than three decades later with a similar oil crisis. Once again, our government that should have been supporting, funding, and endorsing alternative energy was asleep at the wheel, or purposely maybe not. Please keep in mind that the oil lobby is one of the strongest lobbies in Washington and has been for many years. Also, millions of dollars flow consistently from the major oil companies as campaign contributions, which create loyalty and commitments from many of our politicians who also in many cases have a personal vested interest in the major oil companies. For those of you who don't know, 50 years ago a gallon of gasoline sold for $0.28 in the early '60's and rose to more than $4.00 a gallon in 2008 and recently, yet I don't believe that any of the major oil companies just broke even in any given year. In fact, Exxon/Mobil declared record profits of more than $40 billion a few years ago as mentioned earlier. To put this into its proper perspective, there are probably only a handful of companies in the United States that have annual sales of more than $40 billion, yet Exxon/Mobil declared this amount in annual gross profits. Amazing, isn't it? Also, it appears that the other majors announced record profits. So what is wrong with this picture? Only the oil companies and our legislature can possibly answer that question. When you look at the average household income about 50 years ago it was about $5,000 and rose to roughly $50,000 in 2007. This means that the average household income went up tenfold. Now, let's look at a gallon of gas that rose from $0.28 per gallon to more than $4.00 in 2008 and recently. This translates to an increase of 15 times or

50 percent more than the household income. So where is the fairness in this comparison? There is no clear offset or equality with this example, and it is no wonder that every American driver is suffering. Of course in today's times, one can make the argument that a gallon of gas is about $3.50, and pretty much in line with the economy and incomes. However, how long will it stay at $3.50? We as consumers will never know. Rest assured that the oil game is far beyond just supply and demand. In order to prevent future long gas lines, as we had back in 1973-1974 and 1980-1981, we need to move more quickly than ever before to develop a number of measures, and with the fullest support and priority of our Federal government. In light of where our economy is at present, John and Mary Consumer can just about afford a gallon of gas for $2.00 or some type of equivalent fuel alternative today. The timing is critical and it is of the utmost importance for us to move very quickly to address this crisis so that history does not repeat itself ever again.

As concerned and committed Americans, we need to be more vocal with our State representatives and Federal legislators in order to move this process along and avoid a future catastrophe. We should be aiming for total dependency on oil and other energy products from the good old U.S.A. and slightly dependent or nondependent on foreign oil, let's say from Saudi Arabia and Venezuela, just to name a couple of key suppliers. Once upon a time and not that long ago, we were very dependent and relied primarily on the U.S. for our supplies. On yet another note, our top three auto manufacturers should be working diligently at building U.S. autos that can run efficiently on several alternative methods, such as electricity and acidic products, as I have mentioned earlier, and other fuel methods in addition to our traditional oil. Hopefully, this will make our country a greater survivor during any future oil crisis.

VI

How Much Will It Cost for Our Future Prescriptions?

IT IS A REAL PITY when our major newspapers had ads inviting Americans to purchase their drugs in Canada due to the cost and pricing being less than in the U.S. The major drug companies have been enjoying great sales and profits for decades whereas a tremendous number of Americans are suffering and are not able to purchase their desperately needed medications due to the high cost. The drug companies' argument is that they are consistently investing in Research and Development, which is true to some degree; however; if you evaluate their investment in R & D it is very minute in comparison to their annual sales and profits that they generate year after year. No one really knows what percentage of their profits goes into research for better solutions. All we have here is that they're investing a great deal of money into this area and I ask, "compared to what"? No one at the pharmaceutical company level or our Federal government has been able to quantify this claim; therefore, no one really knows the magnitude of the drug companies' commitments.

We as consumers know one thing for certain and that is that we pay dearly at the drug store when we pick up our prescriptions, whether we are insured or uninsured. On that note, once again, in our land of milk and honey, more than 50 million Americans do not have health insurance. This figure represents about 16 percent of our gross population, or almost one out of five Americans. Unfortunately, with hundreds of jobs being lost daily, this figure is currently growing by leaps and bounds with more Americans losing their health coverage due to job losses.

We have heard on TV and read in ad's that it costs about $250 per month to insure the average American, or $3,000 annually if you are in average health. With this in mind, and if we spend $3,000 to insure every one of the 50 million uninsured Americans, our country's annual cost would be undoubtedly quite substantial. However, if you think of what we spent annually in Iraq and Afghanistan, at the rate of $15 billion monthly, our cost per year was almost $180 billion. I am sure that most of you will agree that our return on that money spent was practically zero. Just think, if we were to utilize that sum of money differently, we could insure many of our uninsured Americans and cover a sizable premium cost, plus have additional dollars to invest in our children's education, needed unemployment benefits, or provide help to the elderly who require special care and additional medications. At the end of the day we do have the money to do several of the right things; unfortunately, we are spending it in the wrong places where we will never derive any great benefit. Let me elaborate further on this subject in order to bring even more information to the American public. Once again, the lobbyists in Washington that represent the drug and pharmaceutical industries are a very strong and powerful force with a tremendous influence on our congressional representatives and senators. Also, tremendous contributions are made to many campaign funds favoring our legislators. With this in mind, these special interest groups representing the drug companies ensure that these entities will receive great tax benefits and special concessions in reciprocity. The truth is that this has been going on for years and will continue unless we stop it.

Let's try to put everything into proper perspective. Several years ago one of the largest drug companies set forth to acquire another competitive company at a cost for billions of dollars. I am sure you will agree that these are outrageous acquisition costs, but please understand that this is being done for a reason. For company A to purchase company B, the company's sales, profits, and production have to be of a very high caliber. However, company A is buying company B because of its very lucrative margin of profit, which is why they are paying a premium for the company.

VII

America's Future Drive Time

I T IS OBVIOUS TO PROBABLY every American driver as to what they will be driving or able to afford in the not too distant future. About four years ago, according to several well-known auto publications and research firms, about 70 percent of all U.S. car sales were new car purchases and 30 percent were used vehicle purchases. Today John and Mary Consumer are forced to purchase a used vehicle or maintain their existing vehicle due to tough economic times and conditions.

In 2008 consumers were able to walk into a random dealership showroom and drive away with a brand-new automobile. Additionally, the entire vehicle was financed 100 percent, as was the sales tax, registration, tags, and extended warranty. In other words, they drove away putting no money down and just signing all of the necessary paperwork. Only in America can this take place. In today's times John and Mary Consumer would need to have a 650 credit score, as well as put down 25 to 30 percent on the automobile, and pay the costs separately for the registration, sales tax, tags, and most likely the extended warranty. This is a major paradigm shift that has taken place since 2008. Unfortunately, all economic indicators tell us that this situation will only get worse before it improves. Let's examine the attributes that have contributed to this shift, as well as the main causes.

The primary objective of our three large major auto manufacturers, as well as the foreign makers, was to get as many people into new cars as possible. With this in mind, auto loan programs were designed, and as evidenced today, to enable a person to finance a new vehicle in some cases at 84-month terms or seven years. Please keep in mind that just 35 years ago the longest period to finance a new vehicle was 36 months, and in a few cases 42 months. Also, auto leasing became a very significant part of acquiring a new vehicle during the past 35 years as well.

I remember auto leasing being a major part of all auto transactions while working in California back in the mid '70s, after which it made its way to other parts of the country. In fact, I honestly believe that I was one of the very first people to lease a new car when I was living in New Jersey in 1977. I remember driving out of a Ford showroom with a brand-new Thunderbird in January of 1977. The sticker on the car listed for about $7,200 at that time, and I drove away after only putting down $129 for the entire lease payment and probably $70 for the administrative cost of the dealer's paperwork. I signed a 36-month lease for $129 per month with an allowance of 15,000 miles per year and the ability to purchase the vehicle after 36 months for a residual value of $2,000, and I did in fact make that purchase. At that time it made perfect sense for me to lease versus purchase. While taking on that lease I also sold a 1974 vehicle for $3,000. I used that money as part of a down payment on a new home that I was building, the reason being that the new home would appreciate and the new car, if I were to be purchasing it, would depreciate. Leasing the vehicle was not a difficult decision to make.

Moving ahead in time, leasing became a very large part of how auto manufacturers and dealers were able to deliver new vehicles to the consumer, and they have been very successful in doing so until this point in time in which everything has basically caught up with us. Needless to say, much of what has taken place, particularly over the past 15 years with respect to auto lending and leasing, has been very artificial and that is why we are in the predicament we are in today. As a good example, in late 2008 Chrysler's $30 billion financial leasing facility dried up, therefore Chrysler was not able to provide any new or future leasing auto transactions unless there were other leasing options available. When I read about this development I was shocked to learn that Chrysler was leasing so many Dodge and Chrysler automobiles. One might expect leasing to be more prevalent with Mercedes, BMW, Lexus, Audi, Jaguar, and Infiniti or more high-end vehicles, but certainly not your typical $20,000 to $35,000 vehicle, which fell into the Chrysler category. For those of you who don't know, leasing versus a straight purchase enables John and Mary consumer to drive the car of their affordable choice while having a smaller monthly payment compared to a traditional auto loan, let's say with 48-month terms. This program allows them to acquire that vehicle. Unfortunately, at this point in time no one really knows how future leasing programs will be offered to the consumer as an option to secure a new auto. By the same token, auto loan lending is also questionable in light of our current economy, so we do not know where this situation is headed. Let us shift gears for now and discuss what has happened to our top three automakers, such as GM, Ford, and Chrysler over the past 40 to 50 years, starting with GM. In the late 1950s the company was earning about $1 billion in annual gross profits against their total sales. In less than 50 years GM's stock significantly deteriorated, trading for less than $5 per share. So what went wrong with GM to cause this major downfall? There are a number of contributing factors that have caused this dilemma such as mismanagement, unionization, and not recognizing the types of vehicles that Americans need. GM's upper level management was excessive and overcompensated. In other words, they had too many highly paid chiefs. Additionally, the Indians were compensated to no end. Just think, generally speaking, when an autoworker with a high school diploma earns well over $30 per hour working on a production line that should immediately tell you something is wrong. Based on 2080 working hours per year at $30 per hour, that translates to $62,400 per year, along with a very strong benefits package, not to mention that every employee is highly protected by the United Autoworkers Union. Now compare this to similar employees working for foreign auto makers and you will see that they are paid at least half of your typical General Motors auto worker. One main difference here is that in this comparison there are no unions to contend with, and the upper management of these foreign companies is leaner and meaner and receives far less compensation and fringe benefits.

Once we reorganize all three of our automakers, we stand a great chance in succeeding. At present, all of them are in much better shape compared to 3-4 years ago. However, all three of them could use some overhauling.

Let's start with reducing the average autoworker's pay down to $15 versus $30 per hour. This would be a huge savings annually for GM, just as an example. Secondly, they should downsize the number of upper level executives and adjust their compensation downward to be commensurate with the task that they are truly performing. Thirdly, eliminate the unions who have contributed to too much of today's problems. Lastly, they should build and deliver an outstanding product that every American would be proud to purchase and drive just as we did 40 and 50 years ago. Most importantly, let's make that automobile affordable so that we can sell millions of them. Yes, we can do it if we put our minds to it. I personally believe that our American workers are the best in the world, and once again, if we could put man on the moon, I am confident that we can produce an automobile that is far superior to any foreign vehicle. With the fullest support of our Federal government and every hard-working, concerned American, we can truly make this happen as soon as possible since timing is critical and of the essence for all Americans in today's times and economic climate.

VIII

OUR UNNECESSARY WARS

IN THE PAST NINE YEARS, since we had entered Iraq, close to $1 trillion has been spent on this war. The $64,000 question is what has been our return on the investment we've made? As most of you will probably agree, the answer is zero. In addition to this monetary loss, we have lost more than 4,000 American soldiers, not to mention the thousands of casualties we have encountered. On a much smaller scale, we had a very similar situation with Afghanistan, and once again, for what reason? Of course, one might say to fight terrorism. In summary, we were spending about $15 billion monthly in Iraq and Afghanistan with a zero return on a major American investment that America made. If the truth were known, we have a great deal of terrorism currently taking place right here in our homeland. As an example, prior to 9/11/2001, we had 18 known terrorists planning an attack on our own World Trade Centers and the Pentagon in Washington DC. These terrorists attended our own flight schools where they learned how to fly commercial jets while living in our neighborhoods. In fact, shortly after 9/11, while living in Northern Virginia one of those 18 terrorists had a post office box and was purchasing postage at the same post office where I would go every Saturday to pick up my mail and send packages. I must tell you, this was frightening! He could have been living down the street from me and I would have never known. The point is that we probably have thousands of terrorists throughout our country of which we are unaware. The truth is that they have been here for many years. The difference is that we probably have more today than ever before.

The time has come for us to fully protect our homeland first, which I believe we are not doing, and then attempt to stop terrorism in several of the countries in which our troops are fighting. As an example, we have had over 150,000 American troops in Iraq, yet if we were to research this area; we would find that our Atlantic, Pacific, and Gulf waterways are not adequately protected. I had heard on the news a few years ago that there were many miles of unprotected waterway on the west coast encompassing California, Oregon, and Washington State, with very little protection against intruders. Some rough dollar figures were also mentioned as to what it might cost to protect that entire waterway. The question that we should all raise is, "How and why did we find $12 to $15 billion to invest in Iraq and Afghanistan on a monthly basis, yet we are unable to devote similar monies to secure our Pacific waterway in order to further protect our homeland from both terrorists and illegal immigrants?" Rather than have our military troops fighting in a number of foreign countries in which we as a country derive little or no benefit, our troops' efforts could be better served here in the U.S. by performing a number of greatly needed tasks. One of the most critical needs of our nation is to first protect every mile of waterway encompassing the Atlantic, Pacific, and Gulf of Mexico. This would definitely guard against any enemy intrusion or attack, as well as stop illegal immigrants from entering our country. Obviously, members of our U.S. Army and Marine Corp could perform some of these functions and could notify the proper authorities of any breachments. Also, our Air Force troops could protect against any air attacks, while our U.S. Navy and Coast Guard could help fend off any water attack or takeovers.

It appears that we have an abundance of troops protecting and fighting in many countries where we either do not belong and/or derive little or no benefit or rewards for our services that we so diligently perform. The only return we receive are many casualties and fatalities causing many American families to suffer.

I say let's definitely be a friendly and supportive ally to those countries such as the U.K., who in turn lent support to us and have reciprocated when we have experienced tough times, such as 9/11. I personally think that we should help other countries in times of need; however, our country should come first before any other nation in terms of support for every American citizen and business owner. Putting clothing on our children's backs should be our first priority before we accommodate those in neighboring countries. When you look back in time, you will find that we have helped many countries in times of need and in many life-threatening situations in which we have spent billions of dollars. I'm sure that you will agree that only a handful of countries have reciprocated during critical and crucial situations. I have personally witnessed an imbalance of this, particularly over the past 30 years. Ultimately, we give, give, and give and receive very little in return; this is not fair to us at all. Our Federal government needs to take full responsibility since they ultimately call the shots and place us in situations with other foreign nations for good or bad. On another most sensitive note, we have no business going into any country and trying to change their government, culture, or religious beliefs that have been in place for hundreds and thousands of years. How would we feel if another country or countries came into the U.S. dictating policy and attempting to change our democracy, religious beliefs, culture, etc.? I'm certain that we would handle this with a great deal of offensiveness and retaliation. At present and with our nation's current state of affairs such as our economy, health system, job losses, foreclosures, and the like, it is most important to preserve every dollar that we have and invest in the "Good Old U.S.A.", while taking care of our fellow Americans to the fullest. It is too late to try and recover trillions of dollars we have spent trying to assist many foreign countries that did not truly acknowledge our assistance from a monetary or manpower perspective. However, we can prevent all of this from happening to us once again in the future. Our government has to do a much better job of identifying our true allies, as well as our rivals. We have to approach this like a business. Assume that we own a retail store where we sell hundreds of products. Our goal is to immediately identify which products are selling and which products, for whatever reason, don't sell. Once we establish this, it behooves us to advertise, carry, and sell more of the products that make our cash register ring daily and place very little emphasis on those products that do very little for us in terms of cash return. Doesn't this make perfect sense? The same holds true when offering assistance to others that can certainly appreciate and be thankful and gracious to America for our support, guidance, and friendship. For those who don't, we should have enough intelligence to recognize that and streamline and reduce our future losses early on in the game. Please ask yourself if you would stay in a marriage or a business with a partner if it were not a win/win situation for both parties. It is obvious that we all know the answer to this, which is "no". I am all for extending our generosity to others; however, too many of our American citizens suffer from the lack of medication and health insurance, and a great number are hungry and homeless. America should still be looked upon as the "land of milk and honey" and we should be reliant on our Federal government and American citizens to take care of our fellow man in our homeland. If and when we have residual or excessive income, and once we have taken care of our major obligations and commitments to America, assisting other countries, especially our key allies, should be an area that we support.

IX

America—The Future Business

T HE TIME HAS COME FOR our great nation to be managed and operated in the same manner as a successful business. We are facing some very difficult times with high unemployment, the high cost of food and gasoline, foreclosures, and many uninsured Americans. For those of you who don't know, members of our U.S. House of Representatives in Washington have very little business experience. In fact, many of our representatives are former attorneys. I don't mean to denigrate lawyers, however; I personally feel that they make excellent law practitioners but not very good business people. As an aside, about three years ago, a U.S. jet was forced to land in the Hudson River and more than 150 passengers are still with us today due to the captain and copilot's years of experience. In fact, the pilot had been flying aircraft for more than 35 years. Based on his level of experience, we have all of the passengers alive and with us today. To put it bluntly, you just can't beat that type of experience. Recently a number of companies that were in distress and in financial jeopardy have hired former retired and successful senior executives who are much older to come in and attempt to salvage troubled companies. Obviously, they had younger and probably academically brighter leaders who, in fact, brought the business to its current negative state of affairs, causing that entity to bring in seasoned and experienced leadership who possess both a great degree of intelligence coupled with good day-to-day common sense.

Being a former CEO of two companies that I managed from 1998-2008, as well as the owner and operator of the last company, I spent a great deal of my time bringing both companies that were in distress and financial trouble to a positive and profitable status. I was also able to put hundreds of new people to work and offer them the opportunity to earn a very good living and receive what were considered excellent fringe benefits.

I was very fortunate to sell my previous company in late 2007 after growing the business more than 150 percent within a seven-year time frame and taking very good care of those who assisted me with the growth of the company. Please keep in mind that I'm not trying to impress you; however, I am trying to impress upon you that you can't beat good old experience. There is no stopping anyone who possesses the winning combination of both intelligence and good common sense. This, in itself, is a priceless gift to have. If you study our existing government body in Washington, you'll be able to determine why it takes so long for decisions to be made while moving forward with pressing daily matters and issues at hand, not to mention operating under an antiquated constitution that was formed hundreds of years ago. Let's face it, times have changed drastically; therefore, our leaders who manage our country should move forward with these times. For many years, I have observed the method of operation with respect to our congressmen and senators and how they enter into decisions. It seems as if they have a meeting only to schedule another meeting and that is why it takes a very long time to get bills passed and to make decisions on a day-to-day basis on critical issues affecting every American citizen. Any way you view the existing structure, it does not work well and structural and procedural changes need to be made within the body of our Federal government to ensure our success and survival in these tough and difficult times.

Just think how much would change if we had a good segment of our House of Representatives that were current and former business executives and entrepreneurs. Rest assured that many decisions would be made on a daily basis and things would get done in a more expedient fashion. You see, true business people are very cognizant of time and are money sensitive, therefore, critical bills would be reviewed extensively but within a time line and either approved, declined, or placed aside for more information or research. At least some sort of decision would be made compared to how these bills are currently processed. On another note, day-to-day issues and problems facing our nation would be approached and confronted differently by business people as compared to the high number of nonbusiness members making up our current government structure.

It is evident that many things need to change in Washington to better ensure our future survival. The time has come in which we as Americans have to take action. A good businessperson would ask, for example, the following questions:

- What was our return on investment of $12 billion monthly that was spent in Iraq?
- Why does the same drug with identical ingredients made by two separate manufacturers have such a price difference?

- Should the Internal Revenue Service employ more than 100,000 people, and should our tax system change?
- Why do we have certain lifetime appointments in Washington?
- Since we pay our congressmen and senators as American taxpayers and citizens, how can they be allowed to authorize their own pay increases without asking us?
- Why have we allowed so many illegal immigrants to enter our country?
- What is the benefit of having thousands of lobbyists as compared to 435 representatives in our House of Representatives, a ratio of probably more than 20/1?
- Why are we allowing millions of foreign-made cars to enter our country annually, yet from a fair trade perspective, a small portion of U.S. automobiles are shipped abroad? Where is the fair trade?
- What can we do to mitigate and prevent outsourcing of goods and services?
- Should we excuse and waive what we have lent to several foreign countries? If they can't pay us back, shouldn't they reciprocate in some other way, shape, or form?

Obviously, these are some very good and legitimate questions to which I believe every American deserves an answer. People ask similar questions relative to their respective enterprises because they are always in search of doing a better job and achieving excellence. Over the past decade while owning and operating current and previous businesses, I asked myself a very important question each and every morning before arriving at work, "What weakness or weaknesses exist with my business?" Rest assured that there are always one or several weaknesses. It could be the lack of new sales, operational deficiencies, the need for more and newer technology, the lack of adequate working capital, etc. There is always something that needs replacing or improving, I promise you. Also, I'll speak on behalf of successful well-known leaders that you and I are familiar with who I would venture to say think along these same lines and that is why they are and always have been successful leaders with their respective business enterprises. By the way, I also believe that they would do a great job in Washington as leaders of our country.

To summarize, an organization comprised of great business people, coupled with a top-shelf legal staff, would make up an extraordinary team of legislators to help manage our country in these modern-day times. If this were to take place, I believe that our government body of legislators would surpass their counterparts in every other nation of similarity and place America head and shoulders above every other nation. Let's bring our constitution into the 21st Century and modernize our thought process. After all, we've progressed from a manual environment to a high-tech computer era in less than 30 years. To complement this development, the time has finally come for us to bring many of our necessary processes into the future.

X

Fair Trade at Its Worst

For many years we have allowed millions of automobiles to be imported into our great nation annually, yet only a small fraction of what we produce have been exported to foreign countries. Conversely, a number of foreign business enterprises have purchased a significant number of our commercial and residential properties, particularly in major cities such as New York City, Los Angeles, Chicago and the like, yet we are not allowed to acquire as much as a tool shed in many foreign countries. Where is the fair trade? These are just a few examples of our lack of equality as it relates to our fair trade experience. Who's to blame? Once again, our government handles this process and oversees its day-to-day activities. Fair trade would truly exist if an American-made automobile were exported in exchange for every foreign auto that is imported into the U.S. If I am in the lumber business and you are in the tire business a true fair trade or bartering, as it was years ago, would be a true exchange of $200 of lumber for the equivalent of $200 in tires. I'm sure you'll agree that this is a fair exchange of goods.

If we look back in time, our country has given aid to many countries for a number of decades. Verifiable information will reveal that in very few cases there has been reciprocity by several nations, Yet, in the vast majority of cases we gave, gave, and gave and received very little or nothing in return. I'm certain that you will agree with the unfairness of many of these situations. When times are good for us it is okay to be somewhat liberal with giving out a dollar. Conversely, with our current economic situation we have to preserve every dollar that we have so that we can remain self-reliant and sufficient rather than be dependent on anyone else. How many countries have you seen come to our rescue? Not too many, I'm sure. Granted, several have come forward to lend us money in exchange for some form of collateral; however, how many givers or philanthropists are there? Based on our current state of economic affairs the time has come for us to call in some of our markers. After all, what's fair is fair. There are nations that owe us billions of dollars that haven't paid up. Assume that a country owes us $100 million that we loaned them years ago, and for whatever reason can't pay up. Let's also assume that we haven't forgiven the debt. They should be able to pay back the debt, if not monetarily, then with goods that we can use or resources such as oil, gold, medical supplies, or drugs, just to name a few valuable assets that our country could use. This should be the true methodology of our trading practices in the future so that both parties and countries can experience a win/win relationship. In light of our present economy, with credit drying up and cash being limited, we will probably witness more bartering in exchange for goods and services both domestically and internationally. The timing couldn't be better for us to set a new stage, especially with a sizeable administration in place to do so. Also, our top legislators have to become expert negotiators and traders with foreign nations with whom we're conducting exchanges. We as consumers look for the best interest rate when we're shopping for a new certificate of deposit at a bank or an annuity or a bond. We also look for the best interest rate when shopping for a mortgage or auto loan. So what could be so different when negotiating or trading with foreign countries for goods or services? If I became president of the U.S. and was not very familiar with foreign affairs I would definitely appoint someone who is well experienced and who could handle this position for me. No leader is an expert in every one of their areas of responsibility so they hire or appoint people to perform those tasks.

As it stands, we currently have a great variety of goods and services that can be offered to many foreign countries in exchange for their own comparable offerings. In return, somehow and at some point we should have appointed legislators who are masters at communicating and negotiating on our behalf in order to create fair trade win/win situations for both our country and others, while developing long-term prosperous relationships for everyone involved. Based on our current economic climate, it appears that fair trade will grow and expand as a result of our cash and credit dwindling downward. In addition to this, bartering will soon increase as well. Here, once again, it has to be a win/win situation for all parties and countries engaged in these types of transactions. This process will also call for our top legislators to handle fair trade negotiations so that we become more proficient with the bartering process. In the end, they will likely go hand in hand.

One of our country's most significant needs is oil until such time that alternative energy becomes available to accommodate the number of automobiles in the U.S. Granted, we do have some electric cars running from electricity, as well as some hybrids running from a combination of oil and electricity. Unfortunately, it is not enough to make even a small dent when you consider the huge number of cars and trucks on our roadways. Rather than us paying premium dollars to countries that provide us oil, we should be able to barter our goods, services, or technology, just to name a few offerings, in order for us to preserve our dollars and help those Americans in need. Now more than ever before, we have to cautiously police every one of our dollars and come up with other alternative methods for purchases and exchanges. Even though we've been trading with a number of countries, we also need to search for and develop new strategic alliances in order to maximize all of our trading efforts. Although we do a fair share of trading, it's time for us to proactively pursue additional relationships. If our country continues to follow a path that's becoming more troubling and challenging for all Americans, it makes good sense for us to act sooner rather than later so that we are better covered during more difficult times to come. In addition to our oil requirement, as mentioned earlier, now is the perfect time for us to identify other immediate resources and goods that are needed by America and identify and target those countries with whom we can exchange and build new, far greater relationships and alliances. I'm certain that we can come up with a number of fair trade exchanges that can help us now and in the future.

Let's summarize now by examining why fair trade has not worked fairly and equally for America, particularly over the past decade. As an example, if we import 500,000 automobiles from a certain country in fair trade, we should export 500,000 of our automobiles so that the exchange is a positive experience for both countries. If, in fact, we were not able to deliver our 500,000 automobiles for whatever reason, our strategic alliance partner/country should be able to receive from us other goods or services at the equivalent value of their automobiles that we just accepted. All in all, it should be incumbent on our legislators and negotiators to mandate this type of exchange to satisfy all parties. It appears that we have been extremely liberal with enforcing this type of policy in the past. It is for this very reason that we've experienced unfair trading and exchanging time after time. Accountability is paramount in this case and especially as we move forward. Based on the sensitivity and importance of this critical subject, we need to institute frequent audits in order to ensure that our fair trade policy is followed and properly administered by our Federal government.

XI

LENGTHY PRESIDENTIAL CAMPAIGNS

I F YOU REVIEW OUR MOST recent presidential campaign you might want to ask why a dozen or so candidates were campaigning for more than 18 months prior to the actual election. In less than 30 years we've gone from campaigns that lasted a few short months to those that now continue for 18 plus months as recently evidenced. So what's wrong with this picture? More importantly, why do candidates raise many millions to secure a $400,000 a year job? This doesn't make any sense whatsoever. To make matters worse, several of our presidential candidates were U.S. senators and were campaigning during the entire 18-month period and earning an annual handsome six-figure income while on the campaign trail rather than representing us in Washington. This entire process needs to be modified and streamlined for future elections. When you think of the commitments candidates make in order to get elected, compare that to what promises are truly delivered post-election. I'm sure you'll agree that very few come to fruition. The answer is mainly due to our existing and somewhat antiquated senate and congressional structure that was formed so many years ago. There are times when our nation's leader recommends a particular bill for approval or is confronted with a critical issue, such as our healthcare problem, and the bill is bottlenecked in our congress or senate. Granted, he or she has the ultimate power and ability to veto the bill or override the House; however, from a political point of view, the best scenario is to have an undivided and a majority consensus from all parties.

Now let's talk about campaign contributions and where they come from. A great deal of money comes from America's businesses and from major corporations that are generally huge contributors. Although their generosity is always appreciated, let's also keep in mind the special interest they have and count on from their prospective chosen candidates. Please don't get me wrong. I believe that the elected candidate should serve corporate America and all U.S. businesses as fairly as possible regardless of their size. The problem, of course, is when special consideration is given as a result of exchanging a favor. Overall, the best-case scenario is when the bulk of a candidate's campaign funds are derived from American citizens outside of the business sector. This tends to make the playing field fair and square and leaves very little room for any sort of favoritism from the elected candidate. Hopefully, the next presidential campaign will be shorter in terms of length and far less expensive compared to previous campaigns. Most of you will agree that a time frame, let's say from around May 5th through election-day (generally around November 5th), is ample time for one to campaign, especially if the candidate is a current U.S. senator, congressional representative, or governor. Surely, the vast majority of the candidates' time when not campaigning should be spent doing what we're paying them for, which is representing us at state levels, as well as in Washington. We, as U.S. citizens and taxpayers, should mandate this process, especially since we the people are paying their salaries and expenses. Speaking of expenses, our congressmen and senators' expenses represent a generous portion of their salaried compensation. I guess you might say that they live a pretty good life all in all. In return, Americans should receive fast and significant results based on the daily, weekly, and annual investments that we make in our current legislators, especially for those who have held seats for 20, 25, or 30 years. Granted, some of them have been reelected time after time or term after term; however, several of them have become not only content but also somewhat complacent during that time frame. Please keep in mind that for the most part these are not your usual day-to-day entrepreneurs that have to hunt and fish to find their own food and resources in order to support their families. As a result, our legislators tend to get comfortable because they're assured of their monthly paycheck regardless of how well they perform their jobs. In other words, they're really not too concerned about where their next meal is coming from. Since they're protected, we as American citizens and taxpayers should look at this situation in a different manner. Assume that you and your wife are owners of a business. First and foremost, you are personally responsible for all facets of that business and are personal guarantors for any loans and lines of credit related to that enterprise. Now, let's take a look at the fact that your home, cars, personal bank accounts, and other personal assets are tied to that guarantee. Rest assured that if one or more of your employees is in a position to adversely affect your business or place you in some form of jeopardy that you would cease to employ that person so that you can preserve and save your business in which you have everything invested. These same principles should apply to reviewing our current legislators and we should apply the same actions whenever necessary. They should be held to the similar and high standards to which American businesses hold their employees and not any differently. I firmly believe that every hard-working American is only looking for a fair handshake—nothing more and nothing less—from our government. With respect to the state of our country today, whether it is in a recession or mild depression, accountability of our leaders and legislators becomes even more critical than ever before. Since time is of the greatest essence we must move more swiftly and be able to pivot on a dime when pressing matters confront our country and every one of our dedicated Americans. Our future objective prior to the next presidential election is to band together so that we can deliver a national message in order to preserve the hundreds of millions of dollars that are given in campaign contributions. If we do so, we can invest those dollars wisely to help our senior citizens get the medicine and medical attention they need, feed the homeless, assist our veterans, and further assist small businesses so that they can hire more people, just to name a few good causes. I honestly believe that our money would be spent more wisely in these areas so that all of America could benefit. The time has come to revert back to the 1970s and 1980's era when candidates running for president spent only a few million dollars campaigning during a few short months versus what took place most recently.

XII

DAMAGE CAUSED
BY UNIONS

M ANY YEARS AGO UNIONS WERE formed to help those
employees that worked under very difficult conditions,
primarily in what were known as sweatshops. As an example,
many people worked in apparel manufacturing factories with
work practices that were often cruel. Employees suffered from
heat exhaustion in the summer and endured unbearably cold
temperatures in the winter due to the inadequate heating
and cooling systems that were not regulated properly. They
also worked very long hours with few or no breaks and for
very small wages. In many cases they were treated like robots
and second-class citizens and they had no say whatsoever.
It was indeed a blessing when unions were formed, which
helped save those employees who desperately needed some
form of protection. The formation of unions was absolutely
necessary to aid the American worker. The early unions
represented those in manufacturing jobs, but the unions later
grew to represent those in the transportation, food, teaching,
and airline industries, as well as a host of other industries in
which unions were needed. Unfortunately and as time went
on, things changed and unions became tremendous profiteers

due to union dues paid by the workers. At the same time unions reduced their overall services, which created less of a win/win relationship between the union and the employee. On another note, employees felt well-protected knowing that it would be very difficult to get fired since the union would intervene and save their jobs if they were threatened.

My first personal experience with unions was back in the late '60s when I was working in construction during the summers while attending college. I recall that I had a little extra time while waiting on my next beam to be delivered for placement and I went over to assist one of my fellow workers who was slightly backed up. My foreman obviously saw that I had temporarily left my post to assist my coworker and called me into his trailer office. He proceeded to reprimand me and told me never to leave my post unless I was so instructed by him. I explained that I was only trying to help a man who was getting backed up through no fault of his own and that I didn't mean any harm or mean to upset the applecart. He further pointed out to me that I was only to perform my job regardless of whoever was backed up. On the other hand, no one was allowed to come over and assist me if I fell behind on my job. I accepted the reprimand and later that day I came to realize how unions really worked. If I had been allowed to help my fellow coworker we could have finished that segment of the job about one hour earlier. Unfortunately, my foreman didn't want to see it that way and only wanted to stretch the job out.

A few years later when I started my career I went to work for a large finance company. I happened to work in an office in which 50 percent of our customers worked at the local Ford plant. Every January those employees couldn't wait to get laid off sometime in February for about six to eight weeks due to the production lines being serviced and changed over. While the employees at Ford were laid off they still managed to receive a significant portion of their pay resulting from their union contract. They were ecstatic about this annual event because they could collect their pay while they were laid off and also find part—or full-time work elsewhere to help subsidize their income. By comparison, when other nonunion employees were laid off, they sat in the unemployment line only to collect a small fraction of their normal 40-hour per week pay.

Several years later I was working for TRW Information Services Division and selling financial databases in New York City to major banks and retailers. While working with one of the major New York department stores, I was in for somewhat of a surprise. Prior to going in to make a large presentation I was contacted by one of their Senior Vice Presidents who advised me to be extra careful of what I might say during my presentation since this operation was unionized and that a union representative would be present to represent their employees during my entire visit. Please keep in mind that the system I was selling did not place any of their employees in any sort of jeopardy or threaten their jobs. In fact, my new service would create other opportunities for them in that department store chain. To make a long story short, I made the sale; however, I was quite dismayed and perplexed with this entire union situation. We were a Fortune 100 company selling to one of the largest department store chains in the country yet we had to appease the union that, in essence, had to bless our sale. Although you might think this sounds ridiculous, it really took place. These were just several of my experiences with unionization in three different settings.

Take a good look at what took place with our top three auto manufacturers and why they were in such a financial dilemma. They had an array of issues and problems; however, if we examine their problems in priority order we will probably discover that labor and unionization were major contributors to their situation. The unions such as the UAW, or United Auto Workers Union, that represent automotive workers at the "big three" have been the primary cause and culprit of high employee hourly pay rates. When coupled with above average fringe benefits, it costs G.M., Ford, and Chrysler an exorbitant amount of money, not to mention what it costs to fund pension plans for retired and inactive employees. Even if the average hourly rate per employee is $30, you can probably add another $15 per hour, which is contributed by the company for benefits, effectively driving the rate north of $45 per hour. These costs are obviously factored into the cost of the automobile which, in effect, you and I as consumers pay for when purchasing a brand-new Chevrolet Impala for let's say $30,000 today. Recent research has shown that if the autoworker was earning $15 per hour versus $30, and the employer's benefit match was $7.50 per hour, the modified $22.50 fully burdened hourly rate would have a significant cost impact on that same Chevy Impala. In fact, we would be able to purchase that same vehicle for somewhere around $22,500 to $23,500 or for about 25 to 28 percent less. This is quite a difference when you examine the numbers. On another note, this would help more Americans afford this type of automobile and encourage them to buy American as opposed to foreign due to more appealing pricing. This becomes even more significant to Americans since the average household income in the U.S. has decreased from about $50,000 in 2007 to roughly $45,000 today. Along these same lines, the cost of a new American-made automobile should be commensurate with U.S. household incomes in order to maintain affordability for most consumers. All in all, I believe that the time has come for unions to make changes within their own structure in order to create a win/win relationship between the worker, the business, and the union itself, or be eliminated if, in fact, they are not able to conform to this type of future model. I tend to lean more toward elimination, as opposed to structural modification due to a conversation I overheard years ago. I overheard a unionized schoolteacher tell another schoolteacher, "I can't wait to get tenure with the board of education so I cannot get fired and be well protected."

Another time, I walked into a supermarket to have a sandwich made at the deli counter. When I asked the unionized employee, who appeared to be working behind the counter to make my sandwich, she responded, "I don't make sandwiches even though I can, because this is not my job. My job is only to bring the cold cuts out and put them on display in the refrigerated case." This incident took place in 2002, and I found out later from a reliable source that she was earning about $15 per hour and had been working for that supermarket chain for more than 20 years. Her response to me was pretty shallow. Wouldn't you agree?

Another good example of unionization is when you have workers earning significant hourly rates in a number of industries. In many instances not much less than what a local college professor earns who devoted at least seven years after high school pursuing a formal education. These are just a few examples of the adverse effects unions have on the typical day-to-day employee.

In summary, I'm certain that there is verifiable and statistical data that shows nonunionized employees are much more productive since they're unprotected and fearful of losing their jobs if they don't perform. Also, I feel that daily productivity would increase immensely and complacency would decrease since those unionized employees would behave differently knowing that their jobs are on the line each and every day. America needs more entrepreneurs and people that think on their feet more so today than ever before in order to survive and rebuild our country. The last thing we need are people that continue to think "in the box" or more robotic-types of employees. If we're going to compete globally we need to be on top of our game 24/7, 365 days a year. Our competition is fierce, especially in the automobile and high-tech arenas; therefore, it is imperative that we command 100 percent of every American worker's efforts, commitment, loyalty, and positive vision in order to move ahead and surpass our competition. After all, back in the '50s and '60s we were considered top innovators and producers worldwide. We can do that again if we all pull together. The time has finally come to reorganize our automobile industry, along with other businesses and services by removing any shackles, obstacles, and union constraints placed on America's business and service environment.

XIII

PROTECTING OUR BORDERS

IF WE HAD BEEN PROTECTING our borders, especially for the past ten years, we definitely would not have the tremendous number of illegal immigrants in our country. According to certain news reports that have been disclosed, the illegal immigration figures are literally off the charts. Too many people entering our country, not only throughout the past decade but probably over the past thirty years, has caused an overpopulation situation in the U.S.

This obviously results in not having enough jobs to accommodate everyone, not to mention having to financially support these folks through our welfare system and provide adequate medical coverage for them. This, when it is all said and done, puts tremendous financial strain on the backs of American people who pay for this.

It is obvious that when you have hundreds of thousands of members from our armed forces stationed abroad and defending other nations that we as a country fall short in securing our own borders and waterways. Once again, we pay a dear price for helping some of these nations and derive little or nothing in return while we forfeit the protection of our borders and create a major immigration problem and financial burden for our country. I'm afraid that our "open door" policy has created a major problem for our country and, once again, this burden falls on the backs of U.S. taxpayers. This situation has been mentioned numerous times by the media, as well as by our presidential candidates who saw this as a major U.S. problem. It is time for our state and Federal governments to view this as a very serious matter and take whatever steps are necessary to stop illegal immigration. We should also begin to identify the numerous illegal immigrants here in our homeland and proceed with deportation to send them back to their respective countries. Just think of what it takes for an American citizen attempting to get into a foreign country. First of all, the red tape coupled with the security scrutiny that one has to undergo, keeps those admissions of new entries to a bare minimum. Since we have been considered the "good old United States of America" and the land of opportunity it appears that we've allowed every Tom, Dick, and Jane to enter our country and establish residency. This open door policy has created major problems for our country in the sense that we now have to make jobs available, and in many cases support these entries through our welfare system, as well as make certain that they have medical attention when needed.

I remember about six years ago when my son was in an accident and we had to take him to the emergency room at 1:00 a.m. on a Friday morning. We first had to complete several pages of paperwork while he was bleeding and in pain and provide proof of insurance that we had through Aetna at that time. After we did so, we were sitting in the waiting area for a good hour and twenty minutes before we were called back for treatment. While we were waiting we noticed that a fellow walking in with his wife and child was taken back for treatment immediately. We took notice that he only uttered a few words in English to the admissions attendant since he couldn't speak our language that well. I'll let you folks read into the rest of this scenario, since I don't want to come across as prejudiced or biased in any way, shape or form. However, he didn't appear to be an American citizen, plus I observed that he didn't have an insurance card, yet he and his family were immediately taken back to a room while my son and I continued to wait in the lobby. Unfortunately, you and I both know that this goes on every day in our country and it has to come to a halt. The bottom line is that we are at fault by making special provisions and concessions for our illegal immigrants and in many cases treat American people as second-class citizens.

Another problem that we currently face is overpopulation. In the past 35 years our country has grown to a population of over 300 million as compared to 250 million during the mid-'70s. When you add 50 million plus people within a 35-year time frame you need to have the infrastructure in place in order to accommodate that significant growth. Additionally, we need to provide jobs for these individuals, as well as medical assistance that they will definitely need. Most importantly, we will need to feed all of them, generally through the welfare system, so that they don't starve. This is considered a major responsibility that falls, once again, on the backs of Americans who at the end of the day absorb these major and significant costs, which entail billions of dollars. All in all, our government has not done a very good job of regulating the incoming traffic of people entering the U.S., realizing of course that we as a country will bear this major financial and social responsibility. If you look at other countries you will find that there is a comprehensive process of scrutiny placed on anyone trying to enter their respective country and establish residency and citizenship. On another note, there are a few countries that regulate how many children you can have so that they can adequately manage and balance that country's population. I'm not saying that this is right or wrong; however, it seems that those countries' governments and leaders have a pretty good handle on controlling their ongoing population stream. Although I personally feel in my heart of hearts that we are the best country in the world, I also believe that we should take a page from some of these countries' books and administer those practices at home to help us better balance our scales.

One of the worst issues that we face as a nation is when an illegal immigrant enters our country and gives birth to a child. Once this takes place that child is immediately considered an American citizen and is entitled to all of the same rights as Americans. Additionally, the child and its parents are now eligible for all social benefits such as welfare and medical assistance, as well as a host of other benefits. To make matters worse, the couple proceeds to have two, three, four or more children that we have to support. Let's face it; even if both parents worked, their combined annual income might total less than $50,000. It's pretty obvious that five to six people living in America would find it hard to live and survive on that; therefore, state and welfare assistance would be required to support that family of six and keep them afloat. The point that I am making here is that we need to put certain controls in place in order to minimize this problem, along with a master plan to bring it to a screeching halt. This dilemma is placing a major financial strain on our people and country since we have to cover all of these financial expenses resulting from our existing processes. As a resolution we can begin with tightening up security on all of our borders and placing a limit on how many people we allow into the U.S. on a daily basis.

If we look back in time, many of our grandfathers and great-grandfathers arrived in the U.S. at Ellis Island in New York with little or no money. They hailed from Europe, Asia, and the Far East with spouses and children seeking opportunity in the good old U.S.A. They worked day and night to support their families without ever accepting a welfare or unemployment dollar. In fact, they were so proud of their daily efforts that any form of monetary gift offered to them by the State or Federal government would have been viewed as an embarrassment and somewhat beneath their own beliefs and principals. Our current system, although a very good one by comparison, has promulgated a great deal of complacency and dependency, while creating a weakness in our society, preventing us as a whole from facing and dealing with issues that don't seem right from a standpoint of strength and survival.

Let me try to put a bow around this topic with this example: My wife and I, along with my brother and his wife, were vacationing in Greece during 9/11 in 2001. We had been there for about two weeks, and the night before we were scheduled to return to the states, my wife and I had taken a cab from downtown Athens to our hotel in the suburbs. Upon our arrival at the hotel, the cab driver got out of the cab with us and started to hug me and cry profusely. I paid our fare and we said our good-byes. While entering the hotel lobby my wife noticed that my shirt was wet from the cab driver's tears and she asked me to interpret in English what he was crying about. I explained to her that he was literally begging me to bring him to America so that he could become the best dishwasher in Manhattan. She immediately responded that what I really meant was that he wanted to start out as a dishwasher and then advance to a waiter's position and eventually purchase the restaurant and probably the two buildings adjacent to it. I responded by saying, "Yes, that's true." I also stated that there are certain people that look at life as a burden versus people like me and this cab driver that look at life as an opportunity and that's what makes the difference. Unlike like this cab driver who was looking at life as an opportunity, most Americans would say, "You're kidding when you ask me to wash dishes, aren't you?" I'm certain that most of you know a few people that fall into this category. However, in today's troubled economic times more people will be forced to explore these types of jobs in order to survive.

Overall, our government at all city, state, and Federal levels, coupled with all of our American citizens, have to work harmoniously to protect our borders, as well as every inch of ground in our homeland against illegal immigrants who have made it a point to reside here without establishing citizenship. We also need to work toward identifying unwelcome intruders that need to be deported back to their respective countries.

XIV

WHO CAUSED OUR
CURRENT HOUSING
PROBLEMS?

WHEN YOU EXAMINE THE REAL estate and foreclosure dilemma today one has to focus on what has brought this major problem facing all of America to light. I'd like to state a number of causes, but let me first start by giving you some background. I remember May 15, 2005, vividly for two primary reasons. First, my wife and I purchased a beautiful lot where we built our dream house that we currently occupy and love. Secondly, when we got home that evening and were watching the news, the anchor reported that 48 percent of all real estate transactions in the U.S. were going to the closing table with no money down with 100 percent financing. I couldn't believe what I had just heard. My wife and I looked at one another somewhat in shock. Ironically, about one month prior to this announcement, around April 2005, we had just sold one of our houses and, lo and behold, those buyers arrived at the closing table and purchased our home with no money down. The first check drawn by the first mortgage company represented 80 percent of the sale price. The second check drawn by the second bank was for the difference of 20 percent of the sale price. There you have it: 100 percent financing with no money down. Now here lies the problem. Let's say that the sale price was $250,000 and they financed the entire amount. Based on today's times and what has taken place with the real estate market, in some cases, there is 20 percent depreciation factor, which is not uncommon today. This means that the value of the same house comes in around $200,000 or $50,000 less than the original sale price. Well, history repeated itself for my wife and I when we sold another one of our houses in February of 2007 and guess what? Those buyers also arrived at the closing table with no money down. Once again, 80 percent of the sale price came from the first mortgage company, and yes, you guessed it, the other 20 percent was derived from the second mortgage company for a total of 100 percent financing. Please don't be surprised because roughly 48 percent of all home sales from 2004 to 2007 throughout the country, from what I was told, fell into this category. This obviously translates to millions of home sales around the country and is considered a major epidemic for a great number and percentage of American homeowners. Here again, with home values down, in many cases 20 percent on average, almost all of these homebuyers who purchased with no money down are now confronted with, as an example, a home that they purchased for $400,000 and financed at that full amount that is now valued at $320,000. Yet they still owe close to $400,000 since very little of the principal amount was reduced. Ultimately, this has created a major problem for many American homeowners with quite a number of them now facing foreclosure due to the high number of job losses in our country.

I would venture to say that, particularly over the past 10 years, our real estate and mortgage markets have gone haywire, to put it mildly. It almost seems that anyone who had a pulse and was breathing was granted a mortgage in some way, shape, or form. About four years ago my wife and I were watching the news once again when they were interviewing a schoolteacher from Queens, New York, who was two months behind on her home mortgage and facing possible foreclosure. She was behind two payments totaling $8,000, which meant that her scheduled monthly payment was $4,000. She divulged that the lending institution gave her a $700,000 mortgage and she was earning $38,000 per year. Her response to the newscaster interviewing her was, "I guess the lender felt that I could afford and handle the home and payment, otherwise they wouldn't have extended the mortgage to me." Based on formulas that lenders use as a rule of thumb this lady should not be carrying more than an $888 mortgage payment as compared to the $4,000 payment that she was attempting to handle. While we're on the rule of thumb subject, this is how it works. Mortgage lenders will generally lend 28 percent of your monthly combined income. As an example: Let's assume that Mr. and Mrs. John Consumer have a combined annual income of $100,000 where he earns $60,000 and she earns $40,000. If you divide their $100,000 annual income by 12 months their monthly income is $8,333. When you take a 28 percent factor against their income this means that they can handle a monthly mortgage payment of $2,333. This figure encompasses principal, interest, taxes, and homeowner's insurance or better known by the acronym of PITI. As an aside, prospective homebuyers should have at least six mortgage payments in reserve or in some form of savings in the event that something goes wrong such as a job loss, illness, or other type of mishap. In this case Mr. and Mrs. Consumer should have six payments at $2,333 monthly, or about $14,000 in reserve as a safety net. The problem is that only five percent or five out of 100 American homebuyers have that six months reserve or cushion, while the remaining 95 percent purchase homes and with no reserve! Well, for one, our government and media were constantly promoting that great American dream of home ownership and touting that everyone should own one. Without sounding like and appearing to be old school, I'd like to bring to your attention the way it was just 30 years ago when we had very few foreclosures and a good balance of homeowners and renters. Approximately three decades ago we had only three mortgage products available to our general public. The first product was called a conventional mortgage, which required roughly 30 percent of the sale price as a down payment. At that time if you were to purchase a $50,000 home you needed a down payment of $15,000. The second mortgage product was called a VA mortgage, which is sponsored by the Veterans Administration. If you had served in any four branches of our Armed Forces and were honorably discharged, you were considered a veteran that had served in any of our wars such as Vietnam, Korea, WWII, etc. With this in mind, you were eligible to purchase a new home or a resale with no money down. In the example cited earlier you could purchase that same $50,000 home with no money down. If you qualified, you were only required to pay closing costs, which ranged somewhere between $500 and $1,000. The third and last mortgage product that was available during that time was an FHA mortgage. The FHA acronym stands for Federal Housing Authority, which was the supporting sponsor of that mortgage. If you qualified, you could purchase that same $50,000 home with 10 percent or a $5,000 down payment, plus closing costs of $500 to $1,000. Once again, there you have it. There were only three mortgage products available to Americans. Shortly thereafter, as we entered into the '80s, a number of new and creative mortgage products were offered, especially after 1982 and 1983 when mortgage interest rates were somewhere in the mid 15 to 16 percent range, which meant that many prospective homebuyers could not afford to purchase homes.

Along came the one-, three-, five-, seven-, and 10-year adjustable rate mortgage products, better known as the ARM. Additionally, we saw graduating mortgage products, interest-only, and several others, just to name a few. These new products came along at the right time, enabling more Americans to purchase homes, better known as the "American Dream". These products complemented the existing Conventional, VA, and FHA products mentioned earlier. Needless to say, home sales started to increase throughout the '80s and '90s, which allowed more Americans to get into homes, and foreclosures still remained very low during that era. On yet another note, homes in the early to late-'90s were only appreciating at a rate of five to 10 percent annually. Our society acclimated and became comfortable with this growth pattern. Shortly thereafter, as we got into the 2000s, home values began to soar. I remember purchasing a new home in Northern Virginia in July of 2000. I sold that same home in June 2003 in less than three years for 50 percent more than what I paid for it. That translated to an annual appreciation of almost 17 percent per year or triple the annual growth compared to 1999, just four years earlier. Unfortunately, those days are long gone and will probably not be seen for another five to seven years at best. While we were experiencing tremendous growth of all real estate throughout the country, business was booming for the mortgage industry since they were now offering home equity lines of credit and home improvement loans. This enabled American homeowners to borrow against the equity of their primary residence and receive sizable amounts of cash. This is how those products worked: Let's say John and Mary Consumer have a home valued at $400,000. Assume that they bought the home for $300,000 and had a first mortgage of $270,000. The second mortgage company would lend up to 90 percent of the current home value, or $360,000 on a $400,000 appraised property. They would issue a check to the homeowners for $90,000 or give them a line of credit for $90,000 as a second mortgage. Essentially they took 90 percent of the $400,000 appraised value, which translated to $360,000, less the first mortgage of $270,000, and lent the homeowners the $90,000 difference. Statistically, probably one or two out of 10 homeowners who took second mortgages either invested the $90,000 in secured investments or made improvements to their homes, such as adding an extra room or a swimming pool, or used the money for some other form of home improvement.

Unfortunately, the majority of Americans took that $90,000 and purchased high-end automobiles, boats, fancy watches, and took exotic cruises. Because of their actions it appears that there are a good segment of the homeowners that are facing foreclosure today. These are unfortunate circumstances; however, they are true in nature.

The credit markets became very liberal in terms of extending mortgages, home improvement loans, and lines of credit from 2001 to 2007, meaning most Americans had a pretty good chance of obtaining these funds. This also held true with regard to buying new automobiles, which in many cases, were available at 100 percent financing or liberal leasing programs. Additionally, Americans secured more credit cards than ever before. As an example, just prior to 9/11 the average household credit card debt was about $3,500. By the year 2007 that figure increased to about $9,000 per household or almost three times in six short years. Just as an aside, the average household income throughout the U.S. decreased from around the $50,000 to a lower level. You can clearly see the problem. Today more than 13 million Americans, or roughly 15 percent of all U.S. homeowners, are facing some form of foreclosure or serious delinquency on their mortgage payments. Needless to say, this is a very serious problem facing America today. I do realize that many mortgage lenders are attempting to restructure mortgages for many homeowners in order for them to retain their homes. Just as an example, lower interest rates, coupled with longer payout schedules, will help reduce the homeowner's monthly mortgage payment and, in some cases, quite drastically. Let's assume that a homeowner is currently making a $2,000 monthly mortgage payment based on the existing mortgage product they have, which in many cases is a one-, three-, or five-year ARM. By refinancing that mortgage to a fixed 10-, 20-, or 30-year product with a lower interest rate of perhaps five percent versus seven percent, their monthly payment could be lowered to roughly $1,500, giving the homeowner relief of $500 per month or $6,000 annually. The key here is that the homeowner can comfortably afford the new $1,500 payment. Obviously, if they can't meet this payment schedule, they will be forced into foreclosure.

The major dilemma that most American homeowners are facing today, whether they're facing foreclosure or are in relatively good standing with their lender, is getting refinanced. As an example: John and Mary Consumer purchased their home in 2006 for $400,000. They put down 10 percent, or $40,000, and obtained a mortgage for $360,000. Let's assume that $5,000 in principal was paid down, leaving them a balance of $355,000. They now go out shopping for a new refinance and are confronted with a challenge. Based on current home values that have decreased, in many cases up to 20 percent, that $400,000 home is now appraised at $320,000, assuming the 20 percent reduction factor in value. Please note that John and Mary owe $355,000 on that residence. To make matters worse, most conventional lenders will only lend up to 80 percent of the home's value, better known as the acronym of LTV, or loan to value. In this case they will lend 80 percent of the current market appraisal of that home valued at $320,000, which means the lender will approve a mortgage of $256,000, the loan to value figure. Once again, as mentioned earlier in this example, they currently owe $355,000 on that home. This would mean they would have to come up with the difference of $99,000, plus closing costs of about three percent of the transaction, or roughly $8,000, in order to refinance and close on the new mortgage. I don't believe that John and Mary are capable of doing this, nor do they want to go to the closing table with $107,000 in order to refinance their home.

Now, let's look at yet another scenario with a little light at the end of the tunnel. John and Mary have decided to explore an FHA mortgage in which they are able to get financed at the 90 percent level as opposed to 80 percent mentioned earlier. In this case the FHA-backed lender would be able to lend 90 percent of the $320,000 value, or $288,000. Here again, John and Mary currently owe $355,000; therefore, they again fall short and need to bring $67,000 to the table, plus closing costs of $7,000 or possibly more since it costs slightly more to close an FHA loan. The moral of this little story is that John and Mary are in pretty good standing and are not facing foreclosure; however, look at how difficult it is for them to refinance. Just magnify this to include those homeowners facing foreclosure or are in foreclosure because they missed three consecutive mortgage payments, which automatically places a homeowner in foreclosure. Let's face it; we have a major real estate epidemic in our country today. The answer is not to sit around and blame the lenders, as we are well beyond that at this point. We, as strong Americans, along with state and Federal governments and all mortgage lenders, need to put our heads together and attempt to address and hopefully resolve this major crisis affecting the all-American dream called homeownership.

Here are my personal thoughts and suggestions regarding this matter. I'm speaking as a previous business owner and operator who employed roughly 300 employees and worked feverishly to keep our business afloat and profitable day after day and year after year. Let's focus on bailing out the John and Mary Consumers who are all in somewhat of a bind. I'm sure you'll agree that these folks are far less astute than corporate America and Wall Street. Corporate America such as GM, AIG, and the like, just as an example, has caused the majority of their own problems. The same holds true with the greed on Wall Street that has been going on for years. I firmly believe that everyone requires some sort of assistance; however, from a priority standpoint, our homeowners, with the majority of them being innocent victims, should definitely come first and foremost. The timing for this change is critical in nature, as it will only worsen as time goes on. The truth is that we can't afford to let this go on and must act today in order to help our fellow Americans.

XV

AMERICA'S FUTURE WORKPLACE

F OR THOSE OF US WHO are too young to recall, I'd like to give you a little history based on my knowledge of where America was around the year 1900. From what I am told, our grandfathers and great-grandfathers worked as farmers, merchants, peddlers, barterers, and performed whatever tasks were necessary in order to make a living and support their families. You might classify them as hunters and fishermen who went out daily to bring home the meal in order to feed their wives and children. Most importantly, almost all of them were self-employed in some way, shape, or form and were able to survive. As times changed and manufacturing came into play by the late '60s and early '70s, most Americans were working somewhere in corporate America. This workforce represented more than 65 percent of our working population, while the remaining was self-employed and/or working for the government. As evidenced today, our country is going through a paradigm shift.

As mentioned earlier in this book, over the past few years, more than 25 million working Americans filed 1099 forms with the Internal Revenue Service relating to home-based businesses. That's right, 25 million Americans, or nearly 15 percent of our total working population, are working from home. These self-employed people are engaged in the following areas, just to name a few.

- Medical Billing
- Customer Service
- Telemarketing
- Appointment Setters
- Visiting Nurses
- Insurance
- Sales
- Real Estate
- Web Designers
- Child Care
- Architects and Designers
- Collection Agents

With today's technology and with sophisticated telecom equipment such as computers, fax machines, and other applicable tools, more people are able to work from the comfort of their homes as compared to traveling to a traditional job. It is evident that we will see more of this. With all of the jobs lost daily due to companies downsizing, rightsizing, and outsourcing to India, the Philippines, and other countries, our workforce will be compelled to explore other options in order to survive. In the vast majority of cases, these jobs will not be replicated; therefore, unemployed workers will have no other option other than to explore new opportunities outside of their realm of expertise. To put this mildly, this is called survival.

Around April of 2008, my wife called me in to watch a news broadcast pertaining to students attending a college in

Georgia who were scheduled to graduate the next month. It was frightening to hear what the four students being interviewed had to say. They were all very excited when they entered college as freshman in September of 2004, but were extremely concerned as to what they may encounter after graduating in June of 2008. They were very dismayed at the prospect of finding a job, not necessarily just in their given discipline, but any decent job. Unfortunately, this situation is a big concern of the majority of college graduates nationwide. Today, you have more college graduates working at Burger King, McDonald's, Taco Bell, The Home Depot, Lowe's, and wherever else they can find work. In fact, I'll speculate that only 20 to 25 percent of all college graduates will find employment in their respective fields while the remaining 75 to 80 percent will secure employment wherever they can get it.

After that broadcast my wife asked me what I thought might happen, especially since our son would be graduating from college in the near future. I responded to her that these graduates, including our son, will have to create their own opportunities just like our grandfathers did back in the early 1900s in order to survive. They will need to be self-employed in some type of venture if they can't find work in the traditional employment marketplace. Today, more entrepreneurs are sprouting up all over the country. Most importantly, people are taking a very proactive approach while they are still gainfully employed, knowing that they can receive a pink slip any day, as many Americans have fallen victims to this throughout the past year. New businesses are sprouting up each day with respect to new franchises, Internet opportunities, and a host of new home-based businesses.

On another note, manufacturing needs to be brought back to the U.S. so that thousands of new jobs can be created. Time and time again I've heard that Americans will not work for lower wages, which I believe might have been true four or five years ago; however, that does not seem to be true in today's economic climate. Most Americans are more than happy to have a job and make the necessary adjustments in their lifestyles in order to take care of their families and survive. I can attest to this change in attitude, as I have spoken with a number of people on a daily basis from all levels of life that confirm this. Regardless of income or stature, everyone I meet is watching every one of their dollars very closely. In today's times, "Cash is King", especially since credit is drying up. Most Americans have been living on credit and felt pretty secure with their job. Unfortunately, that is not the case today. Along with manufacturing in the U.S., as mentioned earlier, the time has come to bring back more trade and vocational schools that are affordable to everyone. I can remember while going to public high school that we also had a vocational school in our city that accommodated those students who wanted a trade upon graduating and were not going to attend college or enter into the business world. While attending vocational school they could major in plumbing, welding, auto mechanics, air-conditioning, become an electrician, and so on. By the way, these same crafts and services are much needed today as much as they were 45 years ago when I was in high school. On another note, anyone who is working in these trades today is earning a very decent living. Plumbers, electricians, welders, carpenters, air-conditioning specialists, and the like are making pretty good money and are in demand. I happen to know a few auto mechanics that earn $20 to $25 per hour and have steady work all year long. The point is that not everyone can go to college due to financial drawbacks or the lack of academic credentials; therefore, other inexpensive options such as vocational schools should be made available so they can pursue a career in one of many trades that are currently in demand despite our tough times. Regardless of good times or bad, good trade specialists are always needed. In fact, you'll probably see more people entering these fields than ever before. How many Realtors, mortgage brokers, stockbrokers, insurance and car salespeople are doing well today? The answer is not very many. A number of these folks were earning a consistent six-figure income just a few years ago, and today they are either unemployed or working for a third of their former wages if they are lucky. Subsequently, they're forced to explore other options and industries in order to pay their bills and survive. Some will explore a trade; others will go into the medical field where there is currently a great demand for nurses, technicians, administrators, etc. The remainder will explore small business ventures, home-based businesses of some sort, as well as direct sales, better known as network marketing in which 13 million Americans are employed. For those of you who don't know, the direct sales industry is a $130 billion industry that paid out $65 billion in commissions yearly over the past few years to 55 million sales distributors worldwide. As mentioned earlier, 13 million of those 55 million are working here in the U.S. The direct sales industry has been around for 100 years and has grown at the rate of 10 percent per year, or 100 percent over the past decade. Also, there are bona fide projections that the industry will probably double during the next five to six years due to millions of people joining this industry, which has a lot to offer. There are many business opportunities, including franchises, which are available to today's businessmen and women. Unfortunately, these opportunities require a sizable amount of capital in order to start up or purchase. With respect to direct sales or network marketing, many people started with investments of less than $2,000 and presently earning a good five—and six-figure annual passive income working daily from the comfort of their homes with no major overhead or employees. Today, there are hundreds of good direct sales companies that are doing well and helping millions of people earn good incomes. As an example, Dell Inc. is a direct sales company where you can purchase a customized Dell computer by calling their toll-free number or via the Internet. The company sells directly to the consumer without a middleman and drop-ships the computer right to your doorstep. Also, Dell computers can be purchased in certain retail stores as of lately. Obviously, that is why their prices are so reasonable and affordable. I, as well as members of my household, have taken delivery of several of these mail order computers over the past 10 years and have had a great experience overall. A true direct sales transaction in which the seller provides a product or service directly to the consumer reduces the sale price of that item by about 40 percent. When purchased at a department store or other type of retail environment, the advertising and distribution costs represent roughly 40 percent of the sale price. As an example, a skin care product that sells in a department store or drug store chain such as Walgreens or CVS might sell for $20. About 40 percent of that sale price is considered distribution and advertising costs, or $8 of the $20 price. The remaining 60 percent or $12 is true manufacturing cost, which also includes profit. In other words, if a consumer were to buy a product directly from the manufacturer the purchase price would only be $12. This is called a direct sales transaction. The same holds true to a large degree when you purchase a computer directly from Dell. In doing so, a consumer can probably have a computer directly shipped to their doorstep for let's say $725 that would otherwise sell for about $1,200 if distribution and advertising costs were involved. You will see more direct sales transactions in the future as a result of the thousands of companies sprouting up, with many more

to come that will offer products and services that Americans purchase and use every day.

Now let's talk about another area that will experience significant growth, once again, resulting from our current economy and state of affairs. We will probably see more people entering the four branches of our Armed Forces as they become frustrated with not being able to find employment. Uncle Sam is always in a hiring mode and constantly in search of good men and women. The military will train you in almost any area of expertise. They provide training for a variety of trades including many forms of technology, back-office type work, and in the medical arena, which in today's times is a market very much in need of medical experts. Also, our U.S. military offers a pretty good wage to our troops, as well generous education and tuition packages for discharged soldiers who want to pursue a college education.

There you have it; millions of Americans will be making some very drastic decisions tomorrow with respect to their careers and what they were trained and educated to do. Our fallen economy and circumstances have caused this paradigm shift, sending people searching for other opportunities. I'm a firm believer that Americans are very strong people and will do whatever it takes to survive as long as it is legal and above-board. We will see egos and standards fall to the wayside as our fellow Americans accept the situation at hand and do whatever is necessary to feed their families and survive. I also believe that many lucrative opportunities will emerge as a result of our bad times and that a number of new millionaires will also emerge. All in all, we will survive if we pull together as a nation.

XVI

CONSUMER CREDIT YESTERDAY AND TODAY

WHY ARE SO MANY AMERICANS today in a world of hurt when it comes to personal debt? First, consumer credit debt, as well as delinquency are at an all-time high. The same holds true for personal bankruptcy filings. For the first time ever, consumer debt also relates to both men and women who are under the age of 25. When you look at all credit card types, coupled with outstanding auto loans and leases, the delinquency numbers are literally off the charts. To put it mildly, Americans have gone haywire with the use and misuse of credit. Additionally, we Americans do not save money as compared to many other countries that have much less than us. There is information showing that over the past decade, Americans have saved less than five percent of their household earnings. A number of other countries are saving anywhere from between eight to 15 percent of their incomes, which is certainly a far cry from us by comparison. We are great practitioners of the famous motto "spend, spend, spend", which we do quite well.

You don't need to be an economist or financial expert to understand that when you spend excessively with the use of credit, and save very little, you are heading for trouble. The same holds true for business and government spending, resulting in businesses and our government being in trouble, much like the American consumer. I started my career over forty years ago in the finance industry, and have witnessed all the changes that have taken place with respect to credit. I will share with you why we are in the shape we're in today. Forty years ago the typical consumer had a mortgage that was affordable, a reasonable car payment, which only a small percentage of Americans had, and maybe one or two smaller department store revolving charge accounts. That is a birds-eye view of the way that credit was utilized back then. In looking back, you might say that life was simpler and times were better; a fact to which I can certainly attest.

During that era I can recall the criteria relative to mortgages and the amount of the mortgage payment that one could handle. As a rule of thumb, one week's pay was needed to cover the monthly mortgage payment. Let's assume that your monthly mortgage payment was $250.00. One week's pay should have been $250.00 in order to support that monthly payment. Please keep in mind that back then it was the man's income that was the primary consideration since less than 40 percent of our female population worked. In fact, most mortgages extended during that time were based on the husband's income. Today, both incomes are considered when extending mortgages since roughly 80 percent of women work full—or part-time jobs. The criteria have also evolved from the previous policy of one week's pay to a different formula that we'll talk about later in this chapter. Looking back, once again, in addition to the mortgage payment equivalent to one week's pay, the following formula applied to other credit such as car loans and credit cards. In addition to one week's pay to cover a mortgage, you could take another

10 percent of your monthly income to cover a car payment and credit card payments. As an example: Let's say that you were earning $1,000 per month. You were allowed $100 or 10 percent to cover the auto payment and any credit card payments. To summarize, when a person earned $12,000 per year or roughly $231 weekly, the highest monthly mortgage payment he could carry, including principal, taxes, interest, and homeowner's insurance was $231. In addition to this, they could carry another 10 percent of their monthly income of $1,000, or $100, in order to cover their car payment and credit card debt. All in all, their monthly output for the mortgage, automobile, and credit cards should be $330, or roughly 33 percent of their monthly gross income of $1,000. The end result was that there were very few foreclosures and personal bankruptcies, and in many cases, life was less stressful. As years went by times changed and America was introduced to more credit with Visa, MasterCard, American Express, Discover Card, and Diner's Club. Oil cards such as Shell, BP, and Chevron also became more popular. Additionally, almost every department store, with Sears and JCPenney leading the pack, was extending credit cards to millions of consumers nationwide. Overdraft checking products and other forms of open credit were also introduced. Lengthier auto loans that required less money down came into play on a much larger scale, along with creative auto leasing. To put icing on the cake, mortgage companies and financial institutions brought to the marketplace dozens of new mortgage products to aid the consumer. Needless to say, a tremendous amount of credit activity became available to Americans, particularly over the past 20 or so years. In fact, if you reviewed a typical consumer credit report 25 years ago, it probably contained one page of credit information. Today that same report contains several pages of credit information reflecting all open credit trade

lines, as well as those that were paid off. Please keep in mind that credit when used properly is a very good tool and helps many Americans daily. By the same token, when misused, major problems occur. As an example: Today there are more than 6,000 collection agencies in the U.S. Additionally, there are roughly 2,500 collection attorneys chasing bad debt. When you add the two together there are more than 8,500 collection agencies and attorneys representing thousands of creditors in the banking, retail, medical, utility, telecom, and cablevision industries, just to name a few. Creditors are feeding bad debt that they're not able to collect to more than 8,500 collection agencies and attorneys on a monthly basis. These figures translate to billions of dollars that creditors have to write off monthly since they are not able to collect by themselves. Last year more than $13 billion in fees and commissions were paid by creditors to collection agencies and attorneys to collect their bad debt. That figure has almost doubled from the $7 billion it was just 10 years ago. The bad news is, that $13 billion figure will only increase based on our country's current state of affairs. As we speak, 12 million American homeowners are either seriously delinquent with their mortgages or are in some form of foreclosure. That figure represents well over 11 percent of all homeowners in the U.S. Looking back 30 years ago, the figure was less than two percent, which is quite a significant difference. Now let's examine the problem so that we can focus on the solution. What has brought us to this point in time is the overabundance of credit that is made available to our society, creating a credit environment and a society that is far in debt, for lack of a better explanation.

We have become spoiled and somewhat accustomed to having things now versus the way that we approached life in the past. Up until our most recent economic crisis we could purchase a new home and car, furnish our home with all brand-new furnishings and throw in a swimming pool with no money down or out-of-pocket expense. Ultimately, this became the American way. Purchasing groceries, dining out, taking a cruise, building a wardrobe, purchasing jewelry, gassing up our cars and paying to go to the movies were all done and paid for with the swipe of a credit card and no outlay of cash. Let's face it; somewhere along the way we have to pay for all of these wonderful things, don't we? You can well imagine why we have a major crisis today. Do you think that we would behave this way today if, in fact, we had to put 20 to 30 percent down on a house and 20 percent down on a new automobile as we did back in the late '70s? How about if we didn't have that Visa, MasterCard, Diner's Club, Amex, or Discover card in our wallets? I guess we would have to come up with the cash to acquire these necessities and satisfy our wants, as we did years ago. My opinion and observation is that we will most likely revert back to the past, especially since credit today is drying up in many instances. In a way, that's not a bad thing. Obviously, it worked well for America in the past, which enabled us as a nation to be the largest well-stabilized lender, as compared to the shaky borrowing nation we have become today. Overall, it could be a very good thing for our country if these changes in spending occur.

As a fresh start, we should practice the good old 28/36 rule of thumb, which I will translate for you. In today's times you should only carry a mortgage payment of no more than 28 percent of your combined monthly household income. As an example: Assume that the combined monthly household income of John and Mary Consumer is $10,000. This would mean that they could carry no more than a $2,800 payment. This figure includes principal, interest, taxes, and homeowner's insurance. When you look at a 30-year fixed mortgage and assume that they are purchasing a house for

$500,000 with a down payment of $100,000, they would be borrowing $400,000 for 30 years at a five percent interest rate. In this case, the principal and interest would represent $2,000 and the real estate taxes and homeowner's insurance coverage would make up the $800 difference, making their total monthly payment $2,800. Also, as a safety net, they should have six mortgage payments in reserve after the closing, which equates to $16,800, should something such as a job loss or medical issue occur.

Now let's discuss the other eight percent added to the 28 mortgage factor that brings us to that 36 percent mentioned earlier in the 28/36 example. The remaining eight percent of monthly income of $10,000 or $800 should cover all other monthly payments on automobiles, credit cards, etc. This tells us that John and Mary Consumer should have total monthly payments of $3,600, or 36 percent of their monthly income of $10,000, which would encompass all of their monthly payments including the mortgage and other payments. Let's look at this another way. A $10,000 monthly gross income nets out to be about $7,200 since $2,800 will go to pay income taxes. With this is mind, it enables them to have the remaining $3,600, or 50 percent of net income, to cover savings, food, gas, clothing, as well as all other day-to-day expenses. By the way, this is a great model and template to follow in today's times. Additionally, if they had six payments at $3,600, or $21,600, in reserve to cover all of their monthly fixed credit obligations, chances are that even if something unforeseen should occur they would still be in pretty decent shape as compared to 95 percent of Americans today. I'm almost certain that most of you never learned any of this in high school or college and that's understandable. On the other hand, please allow me to be your coach, advisor, financial instructor, and mentor. I am excited, elated, and care about your current state of affairs, but more importantly, your future, so please feel free to take me with you wherever you go. I'll admit that I don't have all of the answers; however, after 40 years in the finance industry, rest assured that I have many of the answers without sounding like an intellectual bully.

I'm looking forward to sharing more information with you in the near future. Also please look at America's problems today as future opportunities as we take the necessary steps to adjust and move on.

XVII

OUR FUTURE OUTLOOK

ABOUT 30 YEARS AGO THERE were many more renters than homeowners in our country. Additionally, our government felt that every American should have the opportunity to shoot for that all-American dream of owning a home. I firmly believe that both their minds and hearts were in the right place when presenting this to the general public through the media. In the late '80s and throughout the '90s, thousands of lenders felt the same way and developed a variety of mortgage products to help Americans fulfill their dreams. All in all, these programs worked very well and enabled millions of Americans to purchase a home. Many products were introduced, which allowed the prospective homeowner to make a purchase with very little or no money down in many instances. It is unfortunate for many existing homeowners today that the current economic tide has shifted. What we are likely to see in the near future are more apartment renters. This trend will specifically result from two consequences: consumers who can't afford to purchase a home due to the new and more stringent requirements imposed by lenders, as well as those that are in the process of losing their homes or have already suffered that loss, resulting in the fact that both are in need of a place to live. It is clear that we will most likely revert back to times similar to what we experienced some 20 and 30 years ago. This is not necessarily a bad thing since it gives our country time to regroup and create a more favorable blend of both rental housing and home ownership for those Americans who will qualify.

Over the past eight or so years I've seen many traditional garden apartments converted into condos and sold on the open market. In many cases, it enabled the existing apartment renter to purchase that converted condo at a reasonable price. Unfortunately, for many of those purchasers the value has either held to their original acquisition cost or has dropped, causing a deficiency for that owner. Others have increased substantially in value; however, as in any other U.S. real estate market, prices have definitely come down, meaning the owner of that condo or townhouse is forced to hold onto it until better times come in order to sell it at a fair profit.

When it comes to future financing for traditional housing, townhouses, or condominiums, we will probably see financing that requires similar down payments to what we saw a few decades ago. By the same token, there will be some creative and diverse mortgage financing, probably similar to what we've witnessed over the past ten years. Once again, a good balance of both will be imminent. Also, and on a more positive note, we will see home values increase most likely in the long term as opposed to the near future.

Let's shift gears for a moment and look at our future with respect to the automobile market, the second largest investment that Americans make after housing. We spoke earlier about the car market, both new and used, and where we're heading. We are likely to see much more used car activity versus new auto purchases than ever before. First and foremost, recent studies show that Americans today are holding onto their automobile for about seven years. The study also shows that car owners are investing more money to service their cars so that they last longer. Also, with credit becoming tighter, combined with reduced incomes, people will be forced to purchase less expensive automobiles and keep them for a longer period. I can recall that not long ago Americans generally traded in their cars almost every three years. I'm afraid to say that those days are long gone. More used car lots are scheduled to crop up throughout the country, along with another relatively new up-and-coming used car concept known as "Buy Here Pay Here." As a result of consumers not being able to secure credit, as they were able to just a few years ago, along with declining credit scores for those that fell behind in payments due to job losses, illness, or otherwise, they will be forced to purchase a used vehicle and many will also become a "Buy Here Pay Here" customer. At the end of the day, almost every working American needs some form of transportation, which is usually a car.

Granted, many of our new car manufacturers will introduce special pricing and finance programs, but let's see how many people truly qualify. Rest assured that the vast majority, especially over the next few years, will fall into the used car category, which is really not such a bad thing for America as we, once again, regroup.

The third and last category to address is our job market. Many Americans will have to make adjustments with their careers as a result of our economy. There is a great approach we can all take in order to survive. As an example: There were two twin brothers in their late 40s that recently lost their sales jobs at about the same time. One brother, Kevin, sold engineering supplies and Keith, the other twin, sold real estate. Once again, they both found themselves out of work. Kevin, who sold engineering supplies took the position of only selling engineering supplies, and guess what? Ten months later he was still looking for work. Keith, on the other hand, who sold real estate, took the approach that he would sell anything in order to support his family, as long as it was legal and above-board. He took the position of being open to selling cars, insurance, medical supplies, furniture, computers, timeshares, software, food, or whatever was needed to survive. Well, you guessed right. Keith was gainfully employed within 45 days, which is far cry from what happened to his twin brother due to his shallow thinking. The moral of this story is that one brother was non-adaptable while the other brother was diverse and open-minded in order to succeed. A famous quote from the great Vince Lombardi goes as follows, "It is your attitude and not your aptitude that determines your altitude." Keith followed that motto and was successful. There you have it; we have just covered the three most critical areas of survival, which are real estate, automobiles, and careers. All three are essential for us to strive.

I thank all of you for your time, and look forward to speaking with you in my next publication.

Conclusion

I HOPE YOU HAVE ENJOYED all of the information that I included in this book. More importantly, that you have learned a great deal, as much of the information contained here will benefit you. My primary goal was to address each and every American regardless of their current financial or social status and make them more aware of day-to-day challenges that are taking place in our country today. My heart goes out to every American who is struggling to pay their bills and put food on their table. I personally face similar challenges, and probably a few more since my wife was diagnosed with MS some eight years ago. In addition to paying about $10,000 a year for medical insurance coverage for just my wife, we also paid out an additional $5,000 plus for co-payments on medication and doctors' visits last year. Rest assured that $15,000 per year is nothing to sneeze at, but we've had to give up a lot in order to keep my wife of over 42 years going. Please understand that I am not looking for sympathy at this point, but only trying to put things in their proper perspective for you.